Oh, dear! Some of the animals have wandered away from this book altogether! One lion and one zebra (from the North End), one white bird and one turtle (from Faneuil Hall), one hippo (from Fenway Park), and one snake and one prairie dog (from the Museum of Fine Arts) have wandered away from their scenes in this book and onto the World Wide Web—

Visit onthelooseinboston.com

...to see if you can find them there. You'll also find other activities, like pages to print and color, a Boston comic book-making kit, ideas for fun things to do around Boston, and more...

ON THE LOOSE IN BOSTON

A Find-the-Animals Book

Written and Illustrated
by Sage Stossel

Commonwealth Editions
Carlisle, Massachusetts

FOR
MIKE

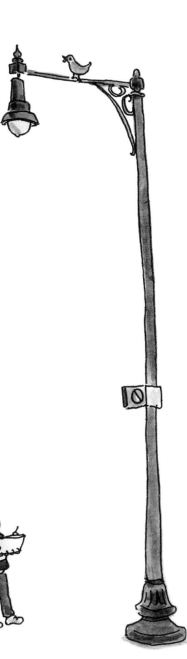

ISBN 978-1-933212-92-0

Designed by John Barnett / 4 Eyes Design

Commonwealth Editions is an imprint of Applewood Books Inc.,
Carlisle, Massachusetts, 01741.
Visit us on the web at www.commonwealtheditions.com.

Visit Sage Stoseel on the web at www.sagestossel.com.

Printed in Korea

10 9 8 7 6 5 4 3

In the city of Boston,
in fair Franklin Park,
sits a snug little zoo
that closes at dark.

One morning the keeper
discovered a note.
"We've gone for a walk,"
the animals wrote.

"Oh, dear," said the keeper,
"what am I to do?
My critters have left me
alone at the zoo!"

The cages, indeed, were all empty that day,
for the creatures, it seemed, had meandered away.

3 monkeys, 2 giraffes, 2 snakes, 2 kangaroos, 2 antelope, 1 elephant, 1 bear, 1 lion, 1 pink bird, 1 red bird, 1 blue bird, 1 yellow bird, and 1 green and yellow bird?

CAN YOU FIND

Then word came from Boston by way of a friend:
A rhino was running around the North End.

1 monkey, 1 zebra, 1 lion, 1 rhinoceros, 1 elephant, 1 moose, 2 snakes, 1 prairie dog, 2 large white birds, and 1 penguin?

CAN YOU FIND

Faneuil Hall called in next with an urgent report:
A monkey was spotted outside the food court!

1 monkey, 2 snakes, 1 bear, 1 penguin, 1 antelope, 1 kangaroo, 1 lemur, 1 tiger, 1 lion, and 2 pinkish-reddish birds?

CAN YOU FIND

A complaint was next lodged by the Esplanade staff:
"Yes, it's true we host concerts, but not for giraffes!"

1 snake, 1 monkey, 2 giraffes, 1 ape, 2 large white birds,
1 kangaroo, 1 lemur, and 1 tiger?

CAN YOU FIND

In Chinatown, then, there arose a small fuss,
for a lemur was spotted in line for the bus.

1 ape, 2 elephants, 2 monkeys, 1 koala bear, 1 camel, 1 owl, 1 antelope, 1 brown bear, 1 kangaroo, 2 lemurs, 1 snake, and 2 large white birds?

CAN YOU FIND

A commotion erupted in Liberty Square
when a businessman's lunch was devoured by a bear.

1 tiger, 2 monkeys, 1 lemur, 1 kangaroo, 1 zebra, 1 large white duck, 2 bears, 2 snakes, and 2 elephants?

The serene Public Garden soon got a bit wild
when a kangaroo hopped right up next to a child.

2 monkeys, 1 alligator, 1 rhinoceros, 1 kangaroo, 2 giraffes, and 1 bear?

CAN YOU FIND THESE ANIMALS NOT FROM THE ZOO: 6 swans, 1 cat, 2 yellow ducks, 1 squirrel, 1 dog on a leash, 2 small red birds, 1 small yellow bird, and 1 purple toy mouse?

CAN YOU FIND

Next door on the Common the scene was absurd,
for the playground was graced by a six-foot-tall bird!

1 bear, 2 large white birds, 1 penguin, 1 lion, 1 camel, 1 monkey, and 1 kangaroo?

CAN YOU FIND

The fans down at Fenway were rather surprised
when a pot-bellied pig chased down several pop flies.

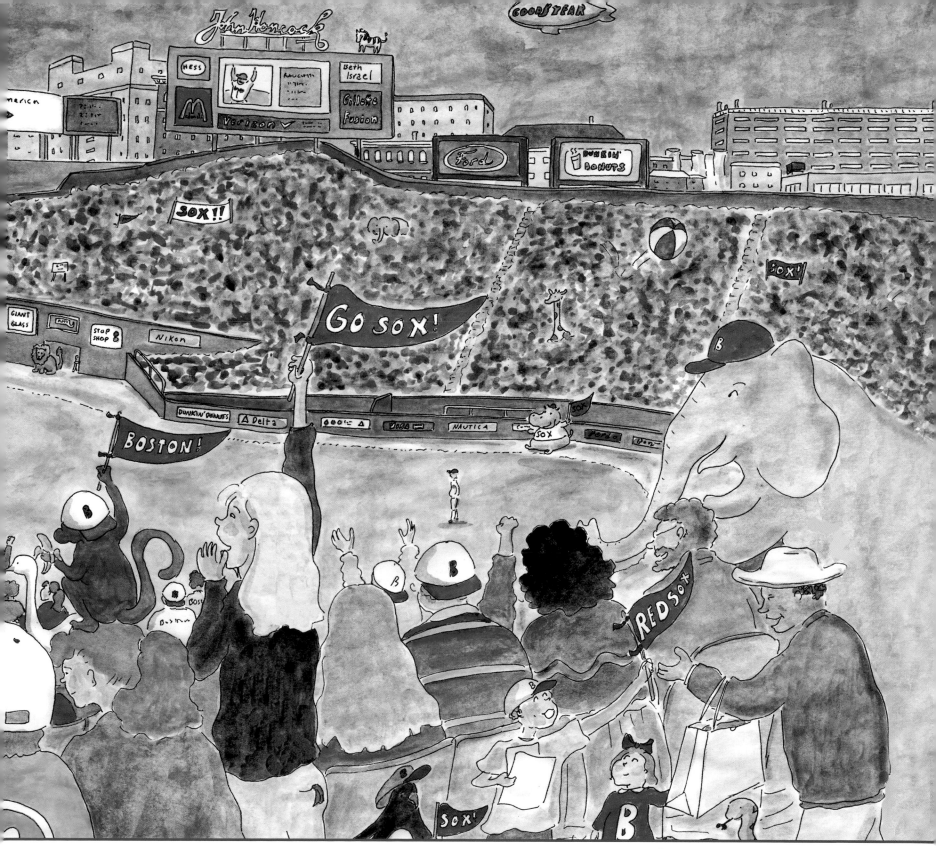

1 koala bear, 2 giraffes, 1 camel, 1 lion, 1 tiger, 1 zebra, 2 monkeys, 1 donkey, 1 turtle, 1 large white bird, 1 alligator, 3 elephants, 1 pig, 1 hippo, 4 snakes, and 1 penguin?

CAN YOU FIND

Reports trickled in then from Newbury Street
that a tiger was sitting in someone's front seat.

1 koala bear, 1 antelope, 1 kangaroo, 1 brown bear, 2 penguins, 2 monkeys, 1 tiger, 1 rhinoceros, 1 turtle, and 1 large white bird?

Then the fine arts museum called in a complaint:
"There are animals here, and they're playing with paint!"

1 snake, 1 ostrich, 3 giraffes, 1 kangaroo, 1 prairie dog, 3 lemurs,
2 monkeys, 1 elephant, 1 parrot, 1 toucan, and 1 tiger?

CAN YOU FIND

When at last night descended,
the zookeeper smiled,
as back through the gate
all his animals filed.

What a wonderful day
they appeared to have had,
but to be back at home
they seemed equally glad.

As for where they had been
they refused to confess,
but the keeper was smart
and could probably guess.